YOUR PET GERBIL

A TRUE BOOK

by

Elaine Landau

Children's Press®
A Division of Grolier Publishing

New York London Hong Kong Sydney
Danbury, Connecticut

Reading Consultant
Linda Cornwell
Learning Resource Consultant
Indiana Department
of Education

Author's Dedication:
For Jerry, Bianca, and
Abraham, who are always in
our thoughts.

A gerbil munches
on a leaf.

Visit Children's Press on the Internet at:
http://publishing.grolier.com

Library of Congress Cataloging-in-Publication Data

Landau, Elaine
    Your pet gerbil / by Elaine Landau.
        p.   cm. — (A True book)
    Includes bibliographical references (p.) and index.
    Contents: Gerbils as pets — Picking out your pet — Gerbil play-
grounds — Your gerbil's home — Feeding — Health care — A word
about wheels — You and your gerbil.
    ISBN 0-516-20384-3 (lib.bdg.)   0-516-26264-5 (pbk.)
    1. Gerbils as pets—Juvenile literature. [1. Gerbils. 2. Pets] I. Title. II.
Series.
SF459.G4L35 1997
636.9'3583—dc21   97–17179
                                                              CIP
                                                              AC

Contents

Gerbils make great pets.

Gerbils as Pets

Have you decided on a gerbil as a pet? You've made a great choice!

Gerbils are ideal pets for several reasons. They are small, so you don't need a big house or a yard to keep a gerbil. Also, gerbils are clean creatures. Unlike many other

A gerbil's small size means it can live happily in a small house or apartment.

pets, they produce only a small amount of waste. And given the proper diet and care, these small, lively rodents usually stay healthy. In fact, gerbils in the wild live in the desert, so they are great survivors.

Gerbils don't cost a fortune, either. While some pedigree dogs cost hundreds—or even thousands—of dollars, gerbils cost only a few dollars. But the best thing about having a gerbil as a pet is the hours of fun you can have together.

Gerbils are wonderfully intelligent and curious. These

Gerbils are intelligent and curious animals.

eager little explorers sniff out every corner of their environment. Gerbils are truly fascinating animals to watch.

Picking Out Your Pet

Gerbils are not hard to find. Most pet stores sell these small, furry pets along with the food and equipment they need.

Buy your gerbil at a clean pet store where the salespeople know a lot about caring for these animals. Don't be afraid to ask questions. As a new pet owner, you are responsible for learning all you can. If the store is very busy on the day you come in and there's no one to help you, go back another day. Never rush into purchasing a pet.

Choose an alert gerbil with a thick, shiny coat. Check its body and tail for cuts or scrapes. Those markings could mean that the animal has been in fights with other

Look for a gerbil
with a shiny coat.

A healthy gerbil has clear eyes.

gerbils, and it may be too aggressive. Make sure that the animal's eyes are clear and bright with no discharge.

Any gerbil may be nervous the first time you hold it, but pass up an animal who tries to bite you or seems unusually skittish.

Once gerbils get used to people, they like to be held.

Gerbils like living with other gerbils.

You must also decide how many gerbils you want. The gerbils sold in pet stores tend to be social animals that enjoy each other's company, so you might want to get more than one. Many people find that keeping a pair of gerbils is ideal. But consider how they'll get along together before you bring them home.

Males might be more likely to fight. Two female gerbils may be best. Be aware that if you purchase a male and female gerbil, they will likely produce offspring. Are you willing to care for even more gerbils?

Your Gerbil's Home

You'll want to provide your gerbil with a comfortable, roomy home. Some people keep their gerbils in fish aquariums so they can be seen clearly from any angle.

If you choose an aquarium, it should be at least 12 inches (30 centimeters) high and large

A large glass tank can be an excellent gerbil home.

enough so that the gerbil can move about and play. Place a wire mesh or screen on top to keep your gerbil from getting out. It will also keep the family cat away from your new pet.

Some gerbil owners set up complex cages for their pets to explore.

Other fine gerbil homes are also available. Most pet stores have a variety of plastic, metal, and wooden cages. Ask a salesperson to help you decide which one to buy.

After you've picked your gerbil's home, you'll need to furnish it. One of the most important things you'll put in it—besides your pet—is the animal's bedding.

Wood shavings make great bedding. It is an inexpensive material that readily absorbs

Cover the bottom of your gerbil's cage with wood shavings.

A gerbil makes a nest for her babies in the bedding.

the small amount of urine gerbils produce. Gerbils will also use wood shavings to make their nests inside their home.

Although gerbils are clean animals, you must help to keep their home clean. Remove the soiled bedding every other day, and clean out your gerbil cage thoroughly every week. Replace the used bedding with fresh wood shavings. A gerbil's environment should always smell fresh and clean.

Gerbil Playgrounds

Gerbils are active creatures who like an interesting environment. Turn your gerbil's cage into a playground by adding a few toys. The small balls, bells, and ladders sold in pet shops will amuse your pet for hours. Gerbils also enjoy most bird toys, and these add variety to your animal's living area.

You can use household objects as toys, too. Place the cardboard tube from a roll of toilet paper in the cage. Gerbils delight in crawling through these tunnels. Wooden thread spools can also be fun. And if you cut two or three holes in a small cardboard box, your pet has a private room to explore in its cage.

Feeding

You will need some feeding tools. Use a small, sturdy dish for your gerbil's food. Some people like ceramic bowls best, but just make sure the dish is heavy enough not to tip over while the animal is eating or scampering about.

Gerbils get most of their water through their food, but

Choose a sturdy food dish (above). A gerbil drinks from a water bottle (right).

always have fresh water available as well. A water bottle with a stainless-steel drinking tube can be attached to your animal's cage. Some cages are designed with a special space to hold the bottle. Drinking water should be changed every two to three days.

Feed your gerbil once a day. It doesn't matter if you do it in the morning, at mid-day, or in the evening, but it is best to establish a feeding schedule and stick to it. Some people feed their gerbils one of the pellet foods designed

Establish a regular feeding
schedule for your gerbil.

for small animals. Adult gerbils enjoy gnawing on these hard pellets, but very young gerbils may have trouble breaking them up into bite-size pieces.

Many gerbil owners feed their pets the prepared gerbil mixes available in pet stores. These provide all the nutrients the animal needs for a well-balanced diet. The mixes generally include wheat, oats, barley and other grains, corn,

A gerbil food mix is a good basis for a well-balanced diet.

peanuts, pumpkin seeds, vegetable flakes, and egg flakes. Most adult gerbils will eat about a tablespoon of this mixture daily.

You can also feed your gerbil foods from your kitchen, but don't count on your gerbil knowing what's best for itself. If not limited to a healthy, restricted diet, these animals often eat too much of their favorite foods, such as sunflower seeds.

Sunflower seeds are fine in a mixture or as a special treat, but too many can make a gerbil fat. It is also important to limit the amount of vegetables

Gerbils love sunflower
seeds, but too many
can make them fat.

Limit the amount of
vegetables you feed
your gerbil.

you feed your gerbil. Small amounts are good for gerbils, but most vegetables have a high water content. Too much water can cause digestive problems in these animals.

If its coat becomes dull and begins to fall out, you'll know that your gerbil is not properly nourished. You can add vitamins for animals to the gerbil's food. If you are worried about your pet's health, ask a veterinarian for advice.

Health Care

While a balanced diet is important for your gerbil's well-being, its health depends on other things, too.

Keep your pet fit. Make sure its cage is large enough for your gerbil to get all the exercise it needs. An inactive gerbil can easily become

Make sure your gerbil has enough space to exercise.

overweight. Such animals
tend to have health problems
and shorter lives.

Sometimes gerbils catch colds. A gerbil with a bad cold might have a runny nose or a discharge from its eyes. It may lose its appetite and be less active than usual.

If you have more than one gerbil, keep the sick animal in a separate cage until it is well again. Set up the second cage as you did the first, making sure to put in plenty of dry wood shavings. Make the sick animal as comfort-

Keep a sick gerbil in a separate cage until it is well.

able as possible. If your gerbil doesn't improve within a few days, talk to a veterinarian.

Keeping a gerbil's cage away from drafts is another way to help your pet stay well. And don't expose your gerbil to extreme temperature changes.

A Word About Wheels

Both gerbils and hamsters love running on exercise wheels, but some wheels can be dangerous for gerbils. Hamsters have only a stub of a tail, but an adult gerbil's tail is almost as long as its body.

A gerbil, pictured here, has a tail much longer than a hamster's.

Some wheels, especially those made of wire, have spaces between the bars that the animal runs on. This is fine for a hamster, but a gerbil's long, fragile tail can get caught in the wheel and be injured.

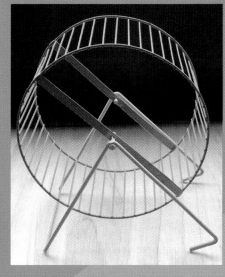

A gerbil's tail can get stuck in the space between the wire in this wheel.

If you get a wheel for your gerbil, make sure it has a solid plastic running surface with no space for its tail to get caught.

The wheel attached to this cage is safe because it has a solid plastic running surface.

You and Your Gerbil

Enjoy your gerbil. It's fun to watch it play with its toys or stand on its hind feet to survey its surroundings.

Your pet will be curious about you, too. Once it gets used to you, it may even climb into your palm when you lower your hand into its

It's fun to watch your gerbil stand up and survey its surroundings.

Caring for gerbils takes some work, but it is well worth it.

cage. A well-cared-for gerbil can live for years and give its owner a great deal of pleasure. You will soon find that the rewards are greater than the work it takes to keep a gerbil as a pet.

To Find Out More

Here are some additional resources to help you learn more about gerbils:

 **Books**

Chrystie, Frances. **Pets: A Comprehensive Handbook for Kids.** Little, Brown, 1995.

Petty, Kate. **Gerbils.** Gloucester Press, 1989.

Pope, Joyce. **Taking Care of Your Gerbils.** Franklin Watts, 1987.

Spoule, Anna. **Gerbils.** Bookwright Press, 1988.

Ziefert, Harriet. **Let's Get a Pet.** Viking, 1993.

Organizations and Online Sites

Acme Pet
http://www.acmepet.com/

Includes useful information on all kinds of animals.

American Society for the Prevention of Cruelty to Animals (ASPCA)
424 East 92nd Street
New York, NY 10128-6804
(212) 876-7700, ext. 4421
http://www.aspca.org/

This organization is dedicated to the prevention of cruelty to animals. They also provide advice and services for caring for all kinds of animals.

Petstation
http://petstation.com/

An online service for pet owners and anyone interested in animals. Includes resources for kids.

Pet Talk
http://www.zmall.com/pet/

An online resource of animal care information.

Important Words

aquarium a glass tank used to keep fish, small animals, or plants

ceramic something made of porcelain or pottery

discharge a watery or slimy substance produced around the eyes, nose, or ears of a sick animal

nutrients the vitamins and minerals needed for growth and good health

pellet animal food that has been molded into a hard round ball

rodent a small gnawing mammal

veterinarian a doctor who treats animals

Index

Meet the Author

Elaine Landau worked as a newspaper reporter, children's book editor, and youth services librarian before becoming a full-time writer. She has written more than ninety books for young people.

Ms. Landau lives in Florida with her husband and son.